WHY WE LOVE HOCKEY

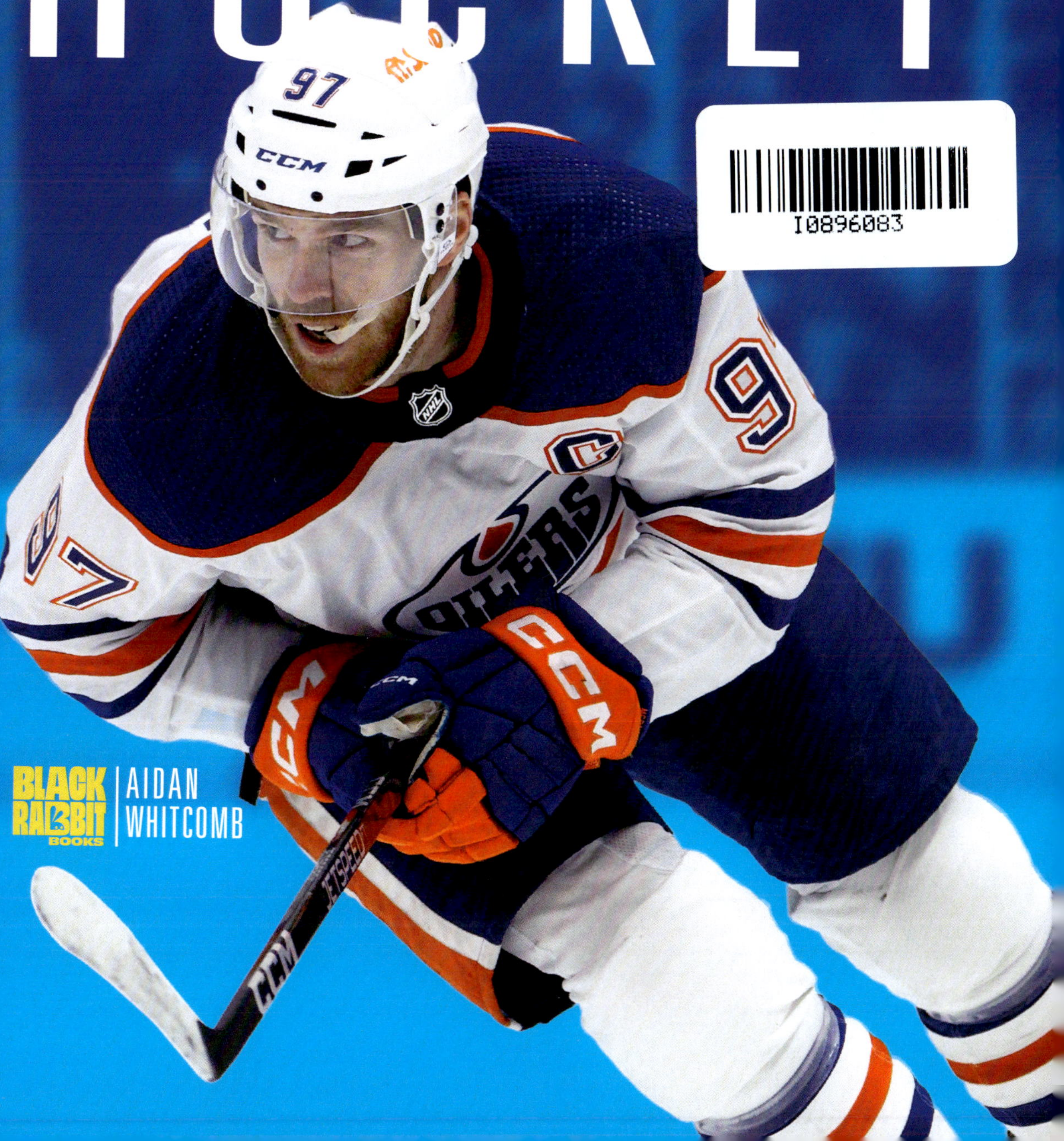

BLACK RABBIT BOOKS

AIDAN WHITCOMB

TABLE OF CONTENTS

1

Icy Origins

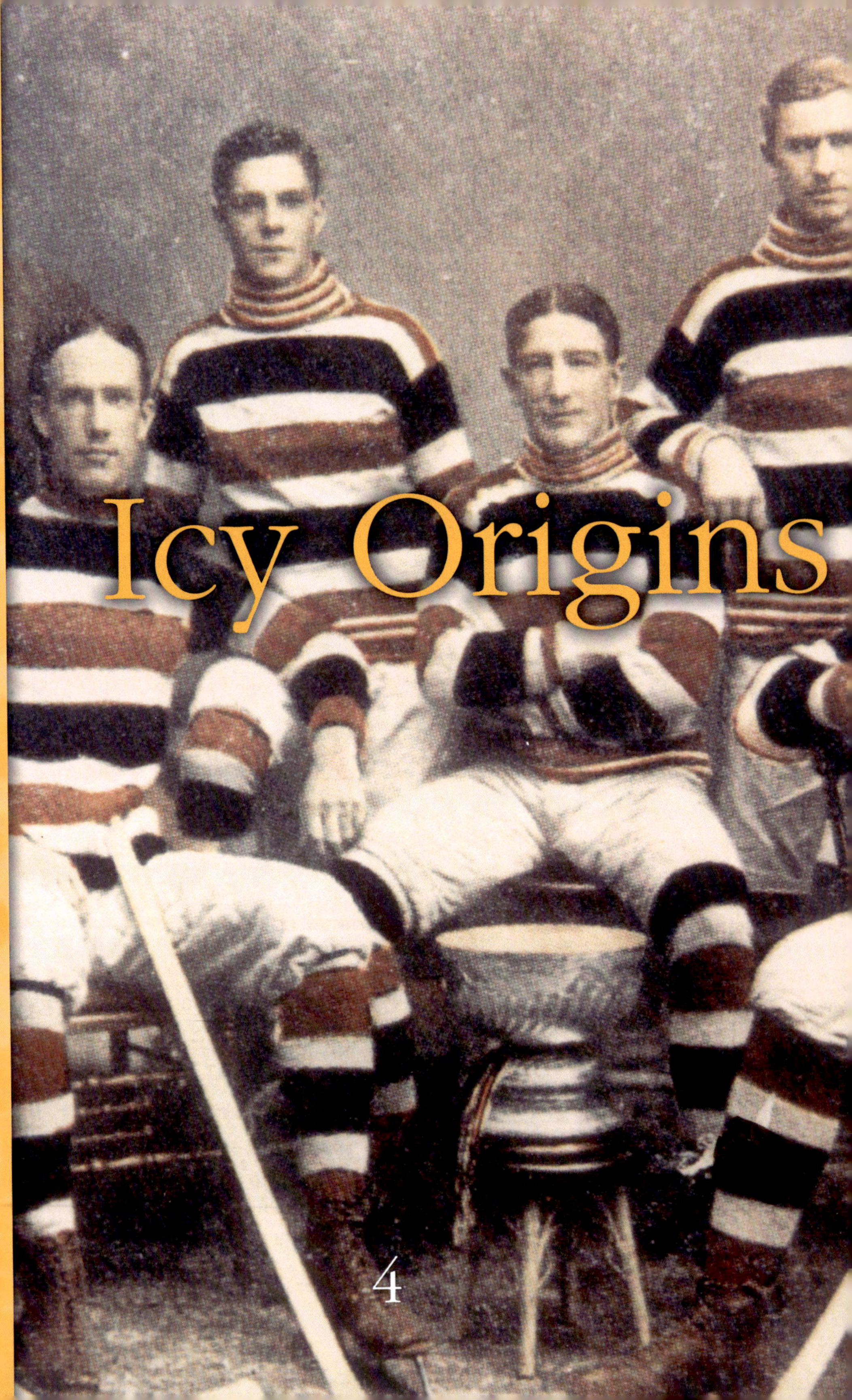

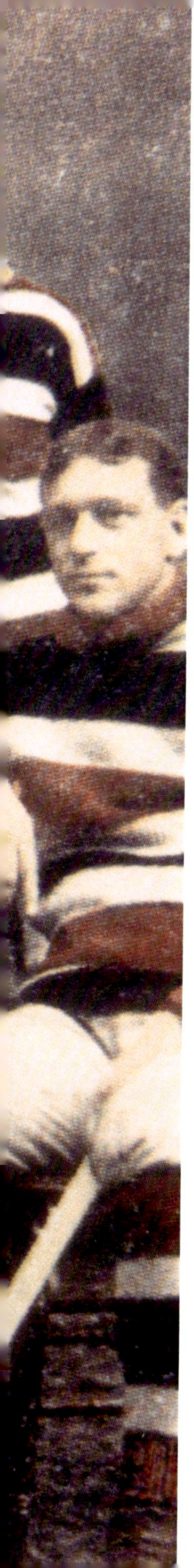

Hockey is a popular sport in colder places. It began in Canada. The first game was in 1875. It spread to the United States. It gained many new fans. People love the icy action and quick plays.

The National Hockey League (NHL) was created in 1917. Today, there are 32 NHL teams. The Professional Women's Hockey League (PWHL) was created in 2023. It has six teams. Fans hope the women's league will be popular, too.

Did You Know?
Hockey is Canada's national sport.

2 In the Arena

Hockey games are exciting. They are full of energy. The arenas are loud—and cold! Fans bundle up to watch the teams skate across the ice. It is an intense sport. There are quick slapshots and rough checks. Players can be aggressive.

Fans cheer for their team. They celebrate their team's goals. They shout the name of the players who score. A player might throw a puck into the stands.

Did You Know?

A hat trick is when a player scores three goals in a game. Fans throw their hats onto the ice.

3

Legends of the Rink

Wayne Gretzky

Hockey fans love watching superstars. Wayne Gretzky is a legendary player. He won nine NHL **MVPs**. That's the most ever! Fans call him "The Great One."

Sidney Crosby is another legend. He has won three NHL championships. Crosby wows fans every time he's on the ice.

Kendall Coyne-Schofield is a women's hockey legend. She skates superfast. She has won six World Championships. Fans think she is one of the best American players.

Think About It
What makes a hockey player legendary?

Kendall Coyne-Schofield

4

Minding the Net

Patrick Roy

Goaltenders are very important players. They stop the other team from scoring. Fans love to watch the NHL's best shot stoppers. They have quick reactions. They need to be focused. Goalies are the last line of defense.

One legendary goalie was Patrick Roy. He made many great saves. Many fans consider him the best goalie ever. Roy won four Stanley Cup titles. He also won the playoffs MVP award three times. That is the most ever!

David Rittich

Think About It
Why is the goaltender one of the most important players?

5

The Stanley Cup

The Stanley Cup is the NHL trophy. It is the oldest sports trophy in North America. The first Stanley Cup champion was in 1893. The Montreal Canadiens have won it 24 times. That is the most of any team!

The trophy has a rich history. Every player to win the Stanley Cup has their name **engraved** on it. There are over 1,300 players' names on the trophy. Many NHL legends have their name on the Cup.

Did You Know? The Stanley Cup is huge!

weight: 34.5 pounds (16 kilograms) • **height:** 3 feet (0.9 meters)

Hockey
in the Olympics

Hockey is played worldwide. The Winter Olympics happen every four years. Both men's and women's hockey compete. Teams USA and Canada have a big **rivalry**.

"Miracle on Ice" is a famous Olympic game. In 1980, USA beat the Soviet Union. It was a major **upset**. The win created a new hockey craze in the United States.

Did You Know?

Hayley Wickenheiser has the most Olympic women's hockey goals and assists with 51.

Team USA celebrates winning the "Miracle on Ice" game.

Hayley Wickenheiser

MORE TO EXPLORE
FANTASTIC FACTS

The Utah Hockey Club is the newest NHL team, joining in 2024.

The first NHL game outside of North America was played in Japan in 1997.

The US and Canada women's hockey teams have medaled in every Olympics they have played in.

Canada has won 14 Olympic gold medals in men's and women's hockey.

Natalie Spooner led the league with 20 goals in the first PWHL season.

Zdeno Chara has the fastest shot in NHL history at 108.8 miles (175 kilometers) per hour.

MORE TO EXPLORE

COOL COMPARISONS

Which NHL players have the most hat tricks?

(as of 2024)

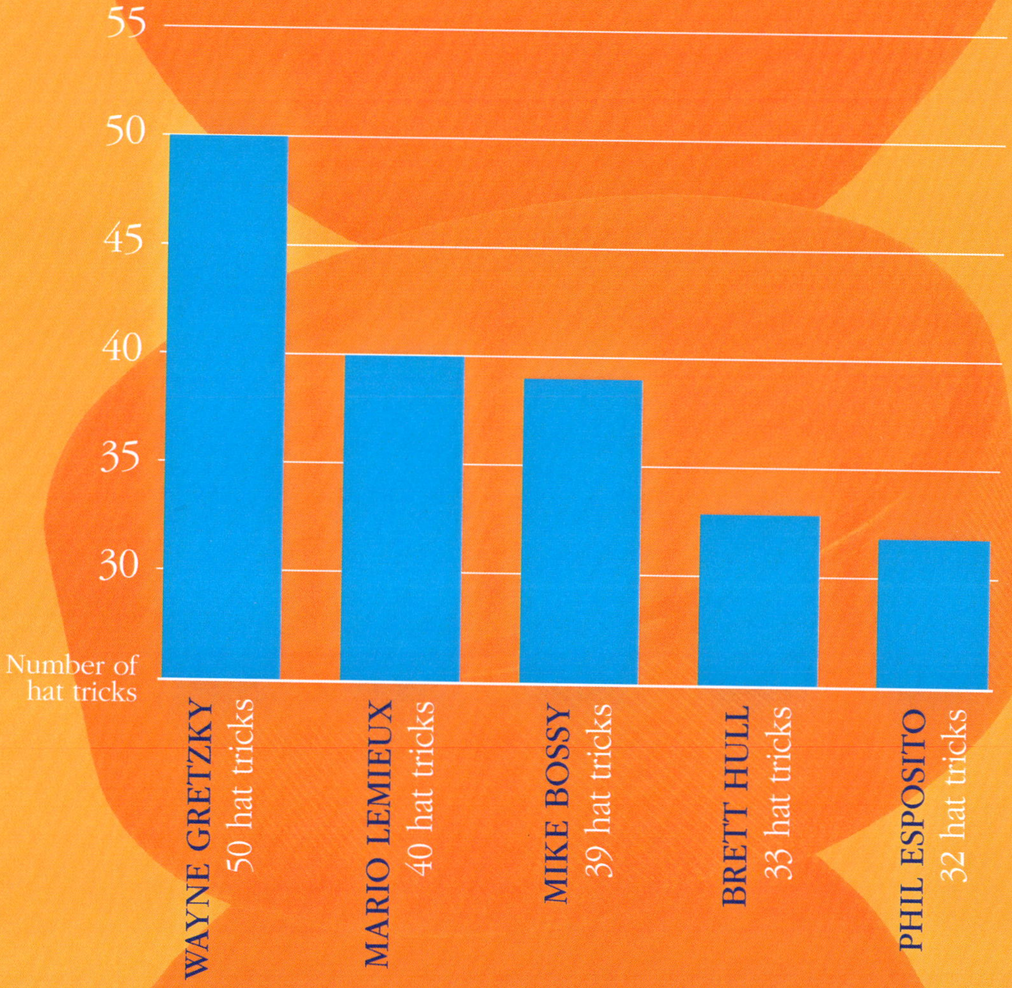

MORE TO EXPLORE

RESOURCES

Glossary

check (CHEK) To stop or hit an opponent in order to steal the puck.

defense (DEE-fens) The players on a team who try to stop the other team from scoring.

engrave (en-GREYV) To cut or carve lines, letters, or a design into a hard surface.

league (LEEG) A group of sports teams that play against each other.

MVP An award given to the best player in the league each season; MVP stands for most valuable player.

rivalry (RAHY-vuhl-ree) The state or situation in which people or groups are competing with each other.

upset (UHP-set) A contest that is won by a person or team that was expected to lose.

Read More

Gish, Ashley. *Ice Hockey*. Mankato, MN: Creative Education and Creative Paperbacks, 2026.

Keppeler, Eric. *Hockey Stars, Stats and Stories*. Buffalo, NY: Enslow Publishing, 2025.

Index

TOP RANK is published by Black Rabbit Books, P.O. Box 227, Mankato, MN, 56002. • COPYRIGHT © 2026 Black Rabbit Books. All rights reserved. No part of this book may be reproduced in any form without written permission from the publisher. • Top Rank is an imprint of Black Rabbit Books. • Designed by Danny Nanos • Photographs © Associated Press/John Crouch/Cal Sport Media, 2, 15, Ric Tapia, cover, 1; Dreamstime/Gemenacom, 5, Vanessa Van Rensburg, 18; Getty Images/Andrew D. Bernstein, 8–9, B Bennett, 4, Brett Holmes/Icon Sportswire, 14, Focus On Sport, 20, John Leyba, 12–13, Troy Parla, 11; Shutterstock/Dmitry Argunov, 6 Grushin, 7, 23, Jai Agnish cover, 1, 10, Luca Santilli, 13, Ridex Official, 16; Wikimedia Commons/Alex Goykhman, 17, Fanny Schertzer, 19, public domain, 21

Library of Congress Cataloging-in-Publication Data: Names: Whitcomb, Aidan, author. | Title: Why we love hockey / by Aidan Whitcomb. | Description: Mankato, MN : Black Rabbit Books, [2026] | Series: Why we love sports | Includes bibliographical references and index. | Ages 8–11 | Grades 2–3 | Identifiers: LCCN 2024050028 | ISBN 9781644668054 (library binding) | ISBN 9781644668375 (paperback) | ISBN 9781644668696 (ebook) | Subjects: LCSH: Hockey—Juvenile literature. | National Hockey League—Juvenile literature. | Classification: LCC GV847.25 .W545 2026 | DDC 796.962/64—dc23/eng/20241203 | LC record available at https://lccn.loc.gov/2024050028